101 Things You to Know About...
SHARKS!

by
Tim O'Shei

kidsbooks

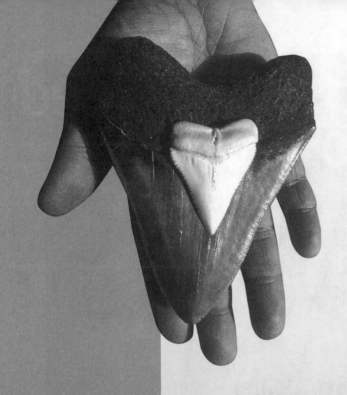

Photo Credits

The Kobal Collection: p. 41
Living Creatures/Dynamic Graphics, Inc.: p. 5
Sea Life/PhotoDisc, Inc.: pp. 13 (bottom),
    22 (bottom), 26, 32-33
Shark Alert/Digital Vision Ltd.: pp. 4, 7, 8, 10,
    14-15, 16-17, 22 (top), 30-31, 35, 36-37,
    38-39, 44-45, 47
Marty Snyderman Image Collection: pp. 9, 11,
    12 (both), 13 (top), 18 (both), 19, 20, 21,
    23, 24 (both), 25 (both), 27, 28, 29, 34, 40,
    42, 43
Under the Sea/Brand X Pictures, © Keith
    Eskanos: p. 48
Visuals Unlimited: cover/p. 3

Copyright © 2004 Kidsbooks, LLC
230 Fifth Avenue
New York, NY 10001

Manufactured in United States of America

0704-1K

Visit us at **www.kidsbooks.com**

 # Introduction

Close your eyes for a moment and imagine a calm summer day. A bright sun shines over a golden beach and blue ocean, and palm trees rustle in a cooling breeze. Swimmers are splashing in the frothy waves.

Then it happens.

First, someone screams. Then all goes silent. Every head turns toward the scream—toward the water. It is a hot day, but everybody seems frozen in place. Every one of them wants to help, but no one knows what to do. A shark's fin is slicing through the water—directly toward a swimmer!

In that scene, we were just pretending. That image is one that comes to mind when most people think about sharks. But there is much more to know. (For instance, not all sharks are dangerous to humans.)

In this book, we have collected 101 facts about sharks: what they are, what they eat, and how they live. We even tell you what to do if you ever find yourself in that imaginary swimmer's scary situation.

Read on, and by the final page, you'll be a shark expert.

Are you ready to learn? Turn the page and let's go for a swim.

Oh, but one warning: Watch out for fins!

The Basics:
The first things you need to know about sharks

One big family

1. There are more than 300 different living species of sharks. Some are quite harmless, including the largest—the whale shark and basking shark. Others, such as the famous great white shark, can be dangerous.

Predators of the sea

2. Sharks are **predators,** which means that they feed on other living creatures—including smaller sharks.

great
white
shark

Just a big fish

3. A shark is a fish. Like other fish, it is cold-blooded, takes oxygen from water through its gills, and swims with fins. Why is this worth mentioning? Because some other sea creatures—whales, dolphins *(below)*, and porpoises—swim with fins, but they are mammals, not fish. Mammals are warm-blooded, and don't have gills. (They get oxygen from air, not from water.)

What makes a shark different from other fish?

Several things distinguish sharks from other fish. If you were to swim alongside a regular fish and then a shark—although we don't recommend this—here are some things that you would notice.

4. You can see a shark's gills. They are the slits on the sides of its body, just behind the head. In most fish, the gills are covered.

5. If you were to rub your hand across a shark's skin, it would feel a little like sandpaper. In fact, it might even cut your hand. Those tiny bumps are called **denticles,** and they protect the shark from being cut by sharp rocks and other hazards. Most fish, on the other hand, have flat scales that form smooth, slippery skin.

6. A shark's fins are stiff and strong. The fins of most fish are flimsy.

The fin-al word

Before we swim forward, though, here are a few more words on fins:

7. When most people think of sharks, they picture a triangular fin cutting through the water's surface—and a crowd of frightened swimmers splashing back to the shore for safety. That well-known fin on a shark's back is called the **dorsal fin.** Sharks have two of them. (The one in front is usually larger than the other.)

8. The **caudal fin** is the tail. Waving it from side to side propels the shark through the water.

9. On its underside, a shark has a pair of **pectoral fins** toward the front of its body and a pair of **pelvic fins** in the middle. These help the shark steer and keep its balance as it swims.

10. Most sharks have an **anal fin** under the tail.

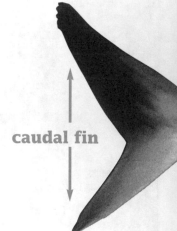

caudal fin

 # A Closer View:
How a shark is built

Male vs. female

11. In most shark species, the female tends to be slightly larger than the male.

No bones about it

12. A shark's skeleton is made of cartilage, a body tissue that is tough and flexible, though not as hard as bone. (Your nose is made of cartilage.)

A sensitive line

13. A shark's senses of hearing and touch come from its **lateral line**—a row of canals that begins in the head and extends straight through to the tail. Lining these cells are tiny hairlike extensions. When those tiny extensions are moved by a vibration in the water, they immediately send a message up and down the shark's lateral line. This is similar to the way a human's spinal cord sends messages from the body to the brain.

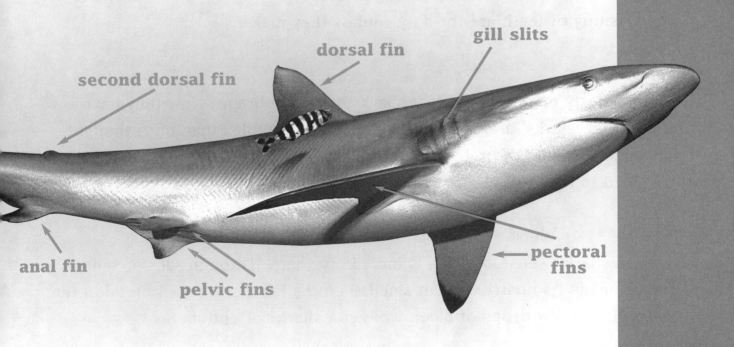

second dorsal fin

dorsal fin

gill slits

anal fin

pelvic fins

pectoral fins

silky shark

great
white
shark

Quiet killers

14. Sharks have no organs that make sound. The dorsal fin slicing through water and the clashing of teeth are the only sounds they make.

On its mind

15. Experts once thought that sharks have tiny brains. Now they have found that sharks' brains are larger and more complex than once thought. The size of a shark's brain in proportion to its body size is similar to that of a bird to its body.

The scent of blood

16. A shark's sense of smell is incredibly sharp. Through sacs of sensory tissue inside its nostrils, it can smell even the faintest trace of blood in the water. Just a few drops of blood will get a shark's attention.

Eye see you!

17. Sharks that live and hunt prey in the open ocean have big eyes and good eyesight. Sharks that live toward the bottom of the ocean tend to have smaller eyes and don't see as well.

Seeing the light

18. Thanks to cells in the eyeballs that reflect light, some sharks have a special ability to see in deep water and at night. Sharks also see in color.

Eye protection

19. Many sharks have an extra eyelid called the **nictitating** *(NIK-tuh-tay-ting)* **membrane.** This is a tough sheet of tissue that covers and protects the eye when necessary, such as when a shark is feeding.

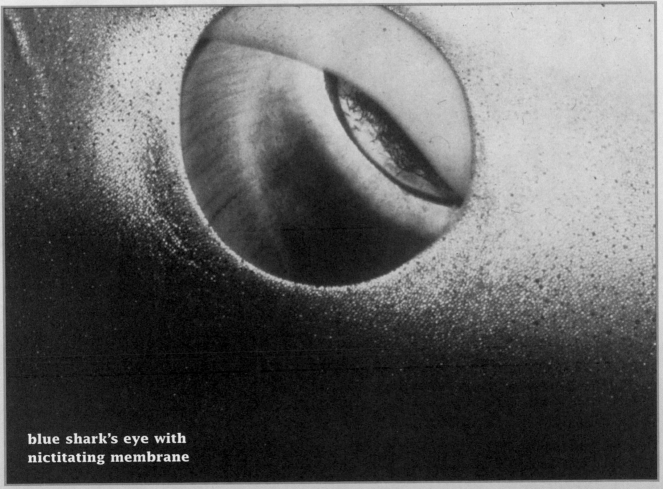

blue shark's eye with nictitating membrane

Meet the Friends and Family

Just swimmin' with my friends . . .

20. Sharks sometimes swim in schools, sometimes on their own. Individual sharks are often accompanied by pilot fish. The species gets its name from the way these fish behave, but they don't swim with sharks to guide them. They are there because they benefit from the shark's size and eating habits. A shark cutting through water creates a current that helps pilot fish move along faster. After a shark feeds, the pilot fish chow down on the leftovers.

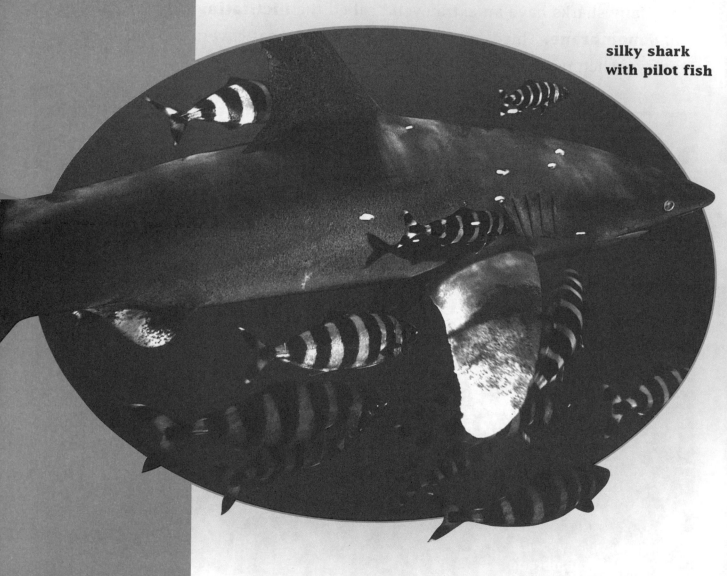

silky shark with pilot fish

remoras on a
whale shark

. . . and parasites

21. Sharks have some traveling companions that, given a
choice, they probably would leave behind. Tiny parasites
called copepods *(KOH-puh-pahdz)* attach themselves to a
shark's fins and gills. (A *parasite* is a creature that lives in,
on, or with another living being, taking advantage of that
living being.) That is an invitation for a larger parasite, the
remora. Remoras (also known as suckerfish or sharksuckers)
latch onto a shark's skin and eat the copepods. The remora
get a meal, and the shark gets rid of some pesky copepods.

Meet Uncle Sharkie

22. In Polynesia and Melanesia, some people believe that their dead family members come back to life as sharks.

Hungry siblings

23. The next time you get in trouble for arguing with your brother or sister, just tell your parents, "Be glad I'm not a sand tiger shark!" Several baby sand tiger sharks develop at once, but the mother gives birth to only one or two pups at a time. The first one or two that are born feed on the others still developing inside the mother, until no siblings are left!

sand tiger shark

Absentee parents

24. Some sharks lay eggs, others give birth to live babies, called pups. After giving birth to pups, a mother shark leaves them. Few of the pups will reach adulthood. Most of them will be eaten by other sharks—perhaps even by their own parents.

Baby talk

25. Some shark species keep the eggs inside their bodies until the pups are ready to hatch. Then they, too, leave the pups behind.

horn shark pup, hatching

The fastest shark

26. Most sharks swim at speeds of 20 to 30 miles per hour. However, experts estimate that the mako shark *(see photo below)* can swim as fast as 50 to 60 miles per hour.

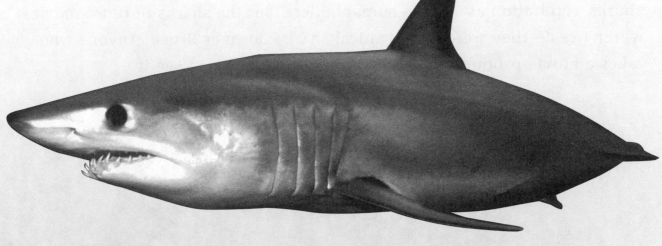

Sharks have good taste

27. As you know, a shark's sense of smell is sharp. So is its sense of taste. A shark has taste buds on its tongue, all over its mouth, and into its throat. We humans have taste buds only on our tongues.

Would you like tuna— or some turtle?

28. Different species of sharks prefer different types of food, but tuna and turtle are popular picks all around.

The truth about <u>Jaws</u>

29. The *Jaws* movies about killer sharks are largely responsible for sharks' reputation as vicious human-killers. But the sharks in those movies weren't real—they were a mechanical shark known as Bruce. Anyone who takes a movie-production tour at Universal Studios can see it.

The real Jaws

The creators of *Jaws* did a good job of picking a deadly predator—the great white shark *(see photo below)*—on which to base their villain.

Here are some facts that you should know about great whites:

30. The great white shark can grow up to 23 feet long.

31. Great whites are usually found in warm waters along the coasts of California, southern Australia, and South Africa, and in the Mediterranean Sea.

32. The great white can swim 25 miles per hour.

you were to count all the teeth inside a great white shark's mouth ould be an exceptionally bad idea), they would number about 300. eat white's idea of a tasty meal would include sea lions, large fish, or dead whales. Great whites will eat other sharks, too.

35. When comparing the bite of a great white shark to that of other creatures, scientists have concluded that the shark's chomping power is more than twice as strong as a lion's. An alligator, however has stronger jaw power than the great white. So would the *Tyrannosaurus rex*, if it were alive today.

36. The great white is the only kind of shark known to stick its head out of the water to look around.

37. Great whites do indeed attack humans.

38. As frightening as great white sharks are, their numbers are slowly dropping. In many parts of the world, it is illegal to catch or kill one.

Home, Shark Home

angel shark

High and low

39. You can find sharks almost anywhere you can go in the ocean—and even in places where you can't go. While many shark species swim near the surface of the water, others stay in the deep, murky parts of the ocean. Angel sharks, many of which look a lot like cat-fish, are bottom-dwellers.

Where the food is

40. Wobbegongs are called carpet sharks because they lie flat on the ocean bottom, blending with their surroundings. This is a useful way to find food. Crabs, lobsters, and other unsuspecting sea creatures are easily caught and eaten by the wobbegong.

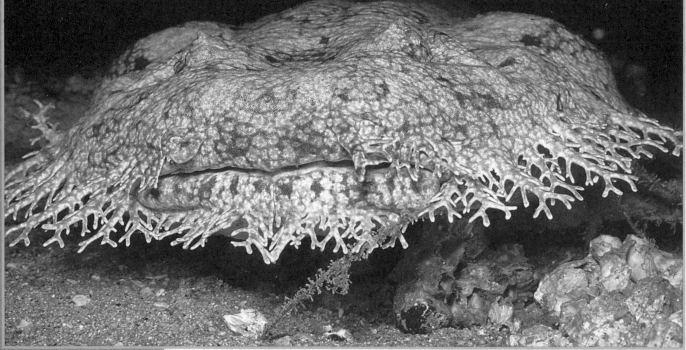

Most like it salty . . .

41. Most sharks live only in salt water.

. . . but not all sharks do

42. The bull shark *(above)* is one of the rare shark species that can live in both salt water and freshwater. It has traveled deep inland via rivers. At times, the bull shark has attacked people who never expected to see a shark in a freshwater river.

Not Just Another Pretty Face

A real sharpshooter

43. A shark is built for the way it lives. No matter how weird a feature may look, you can bet that it's not just decoration. Take the long-nose sawshark, for instance. Its barbels (those two long, slender whiskerlike things) are supersensitive and can detect prey hiding in the seabed. When the prey is found, this shark uses the spikes on its long snout to wham into the prey and injure it, slowing it down enough for the shark to catch and eat it.

blue shark
chasing a school
of mackerel

Hide-and-seek

44. The blue shark is built for stealth and speed. This shark's coloring—dark blue on its top, white on its bottom—helps it seem to disappear against its watery background. Speed comes from the torpedo-shaped snout, which cuts through the water, and the slender body that tapers to a narrow but powerful tail.

Hammer yammer

45. One of the more unusual-looking sharks is the hammerhead. Its eyes are set on opposite ends of a wide, flat head that sticks out from the body. Hammerhead sharks swim and hunt in schools, preying on squid, octopus, and smaller sea creatures. They have attacked humans, but only occasionally.

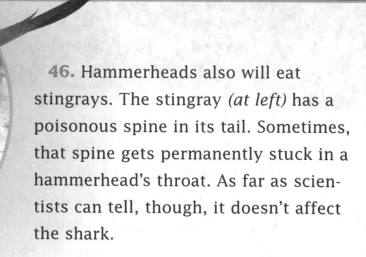

46. Hammerheads also will eat stingrays. The stingray (*at left*) has a poisonous spine in its tail. Sometimes, that spine gets permanently stuck in a hammerhead's throat. As far as scientists can tell, though, it doesn't affect the shark.

47. In the warm waters of the Pacific Ocean, about halfway between Costa Rica and the Galápagos Islands, sits an extinct volcano called Cocos Island. It is a beautiful place, lush with trees. Writer Robert Louis Stevenson called it Treasure Island, and set a book by the same name there. Another writer, Michael Crichton, imagined it as the scene for *Jurassic Park*. It also is known as Island of the Sharks—because more hammerheads gather there than anywhere else in the world.

 # The Long and the Short of It

The biggest shark

48. At 30 to 40 feet in length, the whale shark is the largest living fish. In 1919, one was caught that measured over 60 feet long and weighed roughly 45 tons. (That is 90,000 pounds!) Whale sharks are not dangerous to humans, by the way. They have very small teeth, and eat only plankton and small fish.

whale shark

The smallest sharks

49. Not all sharks are large. The horn shark *(at right)* is only about four feet long. One of the tiniest sharks is named, appropriately, the dwarf shark. The biggest of that species is barely six inches long.

Quick Bites, Part II

Giants of the past

50. *Carcharodon megaladon (kar-KAR-uh-don MEG-uh-luh-don)*, which lived about 16 million years ago, was one big beast. Judging by its fossilized teeth, experts think that this ancestor of today's sharks was 50 to 60 feet long—about three times as large as a great white. Compare their teeth: The small white triangle is a great white's tooth. The large dark one is *Carcharodon*'s!

Not on the menu

51. Shark is on the menu in some seafood restaurants. Blacktip shark, mako shark, and tiger shark are some that you might see on a menu. You won't see the greenland shark listed, though—it is poisonous to humans who eat it!

zebra shark

Get a taste of sharkdom— in complete safety!

52. Around 100 different species of sharks are on display in aquariums around the world. Species most popular with aquarium visitors include the blacktip shark, bull shark, sandbar shark, sand tiger shark, whitetip shark, and zebra shark.

Meet the folks . . .

53. Sharks' closest relatives in the sea are rays—both have skeletons made of cartilage. They don't look much alike, though. While most sharks are shaped like torpedoes, rays look more like blankets.

. . . a whole lot of them!

54. The number of species of rays—around 700—is almost double that of sharks.

manta ray

Chow Time!

Attack cues

Lots of cues let sharks know when to launch a precise attack on their prey.

sand tiger (or gray nurse) shark

55. A fish struggling under water makes a low-frequency vibration, which sharks are very good at hearing. Fishermen trying to catch sharks sometimes use this to their advantage. They create a low-frequency vibration—by rattling coconut shells underwater, for example. Sharks show up, expecting a meal.

56. The sound of a fish splashing near the water's surface is another cue. The shark will detect that sound and swim toward it.

57. The scent of blood is a major cue. The closer a shark gets to blood, the better it can follow the smell of that blood—and track the prey that is bleeding.

58. When a shark reaches its prey, its sharp senses detect another cue. The heartbeat of a living organism sends off small electric impulses. A shark can sense those and use them to zoom to the exact location of its dinner.

A powerful bite

59. When a shark bites down, the pressure of tooth on tooth can be as high as 18 tons per square inch! But the real power of a shark's bite is the sharpness of its teeth (think of a mouthful of sharp nails!), and the speed at which they snap together.

Poor table manners?

60. A shark's jaws can move in only one way: up and down. Since they can't move their jaws side to side as well, sharks don't chew their food, they shake it. When a shark bites into a large animal, it clamps down its jaws and shakes its head back and forth until it rips out a chunk of meat.

blue shark eating a mackerel

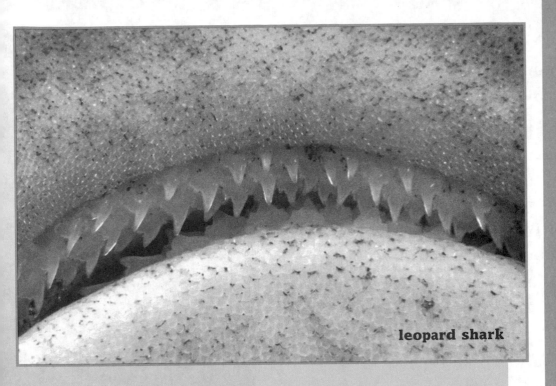

leopard shark

Teeth, teeth, and more teeth

61. A shark's mouth has 2 to 3 rows of teeth, with 24 to 26 in each row of the upper jaw and 22 to 24 in each row of the lower jaw.

Take a bite of this!

62. Different species of sharks have different types of teeth, depending on the type of food they eat. Some have teeth shaped like razors, others have teeth like saws.

Is little sharkie teething?

63. Like a human baby who is teething, a shark grows new teeth to replace the old ones. Sharks do this all life long, though, with each tooth being replaced every 9 to 36 days. This replaces teeth that get lost or broken, or that would become dull with constant use. A single shark can grow 24,000 teeth in its lifetime.

Loose lips

64. A shark can unhinge its jaws from its skull, allowing it to open its mouth wide and far in order to capture a big meal.

Time for dinner!

65. How often does a shark eat? Most have a meal every day or two. Great white sharks, however, have been found to scarf down a big meal—a whale, for instance—then not eat again for two months!

Liver works

66. Many animals (including humans) create body fat as a way to store extra fuel. A shark doesn't have fat, though. Its excess calories are turned into oil, which is stored in the liver.

Floating on oil

67. Put oil in water, and what happens? It floats. Because sharks store oil in their livers, they float, too. Many fish have air sacs to help them stay afloat, but sharks do not. Without its oil, a shark would be nothing more than a sharp-toothed hunk of cartilage sinking to the ocean floor.

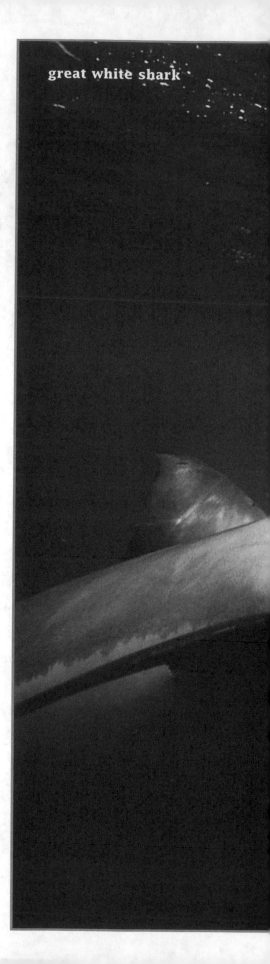

great white shark

An interesting menu

68. The juices in a shark's stomach are so strong, they can digest almost any-thing—including metal. Among the items that have been found in sharks' stom-achs are license plates, shoes, cigarette packs, coils of wire, and a keg of nails!

Unwanted food

69. Like people, sharks can regurgitate—throw up. When a shark swallows something that it doesn't want, its stomach can push the food back through the throat and out of the mouth.

Throwing up on the enemy

70. Sharks have what you might call an interesting strategy for distracting other predators. If, for example, a large shark is zeroing in on a smaller one, the about-to-be-eaten shark may throw up in the face of the bigger one. While the cloud of food provides cover, the smaller shark darts away, leaving the big shark behind to munch on the scraps. Along with get-ting rid of a yucky meal, vomiting gives the shark a way to protect itself from larger sharks that might prey on it.

leopard
shark

Up close and personal

The only way to study sharks is to get close to them, which is not an easy thing to do. Here are three ways scientists manage to observe sharks without losing their heads.

71. Divers wear a special suit made of a stainless-steel material called chain mail *(below)*. Like the tunics that knights used to wear for jousting, it is made up of many small, connected metal rings. Chain-mail diving suits are strong enough to keep most sharks from breaking through the skin, but they won't prevent a really bad bruise.

72. If sharks get too close or combative for comfort, some divers use a protective oceanic device (POD). When this gizmo is turned on, it sends out a frenzy of electrical impulses that confuse sharks and drive them away.

73. To experience a shark attack and live to tell about it, some divers go under the water in steel cages strong enough to withstand even a great white's bite!

blue shark

great
white
shark

Shark Attack!

Three types of attacks

A shark researcher named George Burgess has identified three types of shark attacks:

74. In a **hit-and-run attack,** the shark mistakes a human for food. After one bite, the shark realizes its mistake and leaves.

75. In a **bump-and-bite attack,** the shark first bumps its victim, then swims back and rears for a full attack.

76. In a **sneak attack,** the shark bites without any warning at all. This often happens after shipwrecks and plane wrecks.

great white shark

great white shark

Tips for avoiding a shark attack

There is no guaranteed way to avoid or escape from an attacking shark. However, if you are going to go in the water in an area where sharks might be, experts offer these 10 tips. They are worth a try.

77. Swim in groups. Sharks are more likely to go after a single swimmer.

78. Stay close to shore. Sharks can attack in very shallow water, but you'll have a better chance of getting ashore quickly.

79. Swim during the daytime, not at dusk or in the dark. Sharks are more active when it is dark.

80. Sharks can smell even the tiniest drop of blood. If you are bleeding, don't go in the water.

81. Take off any jewelry before you go in the water. To a shark, anything shiny looks like a fish's scales.

82. Sharks see bright flashes very well, so light clothing or unevenly tanned skin can attract them. This is especially true in murky water.

bull
sharks

83. Don't swim near people who are fishing. Their bait can attract sharks that may go for you instead.

84. Don't splash about too much. Sharks can easily see the churned-up water, and zoom in your direction.

85. Keep your pets out of the water. To a shark, they will look like bait.

86. Sharks can get caught between sandbars during the low tide. They also hang out near steep drop-offs in the water. Avoid such places!

The danger

87. Any shark bite, even a tiny nip, is serious. Bacteria from a shark's mouth can cause a nasty infection, so it is important to visit a hospital right away.

Hit 'em with your best shot

88. Let's say that you were swimming in the ocean and a shark was about to attack you. There is no time to swim away and no one to rescue you. What should you do? Punch that shark right in the nose! Bumping noses is how sharks tell each other not to bite.

Guarding the beach

89. One method used to keep sharks away from beaches that people regularly visit is to secure an underwater net around the perimeter of the swimming area. This works, but it isn't foolproof. Since water levels are always changing, it is impossible to completely block off a beach.

scene from the movie *Jaws*

Survival rate

90. If you *are* attacked, what are your chances? About 80 percent of people attacked by sharks survive the ordeal.

41

The injury to this blue shark's mouth probably happened when the shark got tangled in fishing equipment.

Sharks should be afraid of you!

91. Which is deadlier: humans or sharks? The answer is humans. Each year, people kill about 100 million sharks. Sharks, on the other hand, kill only about 100 people each year. That gives sharks a good reason to be afraid of you—but they don't know that.

Few enemies

92. Aside from humans, sharks have only one other predator: bigger sharks!

Shark Uses

Healthy creatures

93. Sharks are remarkably healthy creatures. Very few of them suffer from bacterial diseases, cancer, or other illnesses. Scientists have been studying sharks to find clues that may help cure human diseases.

lemon shark

Skin replacement

94. Shark cartilage can be used to make artificial skin, for people who have suffered bad burns.

Oily uses

95. Shark-liver oil is rich in vitamin A and squalene *(SKWAH-leen)*, which makes it useful to humans in many ways. Vitamin A helps our eyesight. Squalene is useful in skin-care products and some types of medicine.

Shark eyes

96. Doctors have transplanted shark corneas into human eyes!

Skin(ny) stuff

97. Sharkskin's rough scales make it useful as sandpaper. If the scales are removed, the skin can be used to make leather products, such as jackets, belts, and shoes.

Acne attack

98. Did you know that sharks attack pimples? Scientists have found that a substance in shark bile (the stomach juices that help a shark digest its food) can help clear up acne in humans.

silky shark

Hey, you look "shark"!

99. Some people use shark teeth to make jewelry, such as necklaces. (That probably is the only way you wouldn't mind having a shark fastened to your neck!)

In the soup

100. Shark-fin soup has been made in China for more than 2,000 years. One way of getting the fins for the soup is called *finning.* That is when fishermen cut the fins off of sharks and sell them. Sometimes, however, fishermen throw the live shark back into the water. Unable to swim, it suffers a slow, painful death.

The Last Word

101. Sharks can be both dangerous and useful, but many people insist that they should not be hunted. Sharks left alone are beautiful, mysterious creatures—perfectly built to thrive and survive.

Shark Quiz: How sharp are you?

1. How is a shark different from other fish?
   a. All sharks live in salt water.
   b. Many sharks lay eggs.
   c. Sharks breathe through gills.
   d. Sharks' fins are stiff and strong.

2. Which of these is the fin on a shark's back—the one that sticks out of the water when the animal is swimming near the surface?
   a. the anal fin
   b. the caudal fin
   c. the dorsal fin
   d. the pectoral fin

3. Which of these is among the types of fish that swim along with sharks and help them?
   a. copepods
   b. pilot fish
   c. remoras
   d. both *a* and *c*
   e. both *b* and *c*

4. Which is the fastest type of shark?
   a. the great white shark
   b. the hammerhead shark
   c. the mako shark
   d. the whale shark

5. Which type of shark was featured in the *Jaws* movies?
   a. the bull shark
   b. the great white shark
   c. the sand tiger shark
   d. the wobbegong

6. Which animal is the shark's closest relative?
   a. the dolphin
   b. the lizard
   c. the ray
   d. the seal

7. How often do most sharks eat?
   a. once every hour
   b. twice a day
   c. once every day or two
   d. once every week or two

8. Which of the following helps
sharks stay afloat?
a. air sacs
b. cartilage
c. nictitating membranes
d. oil

9. If you are being attacked by a
shark and absolutely can't get
away, what is the best thing to do?
a. curl up into a ball
b. kick it in the stomach
c. punch it in the nose
d. try to pry its jaws open

10. A substance that comes from
shark bile can be used to treat
which human condition?
a. acne
b. broken bones
c. headaches
d. stomachaches

silvertip
shark

whitetip reef shark